Discover Airplanes

by Amanda Trane

© 2017 by Amanda Trane
ISBN: 978-1-53240-2517
eISBN: 978-1-53240-2524
Images licensed from Fotolia.com
All rights reserved.
No portion of this book may be reproduced
without express permission of the publisher.
First Edition
Published in the United States by
Xist Publishing
www.xistpublishing.com
PO Box 61593 Irvine, CA 92602

There are many different kinds of planes. All planes have wings.

All planes have a cockpit. A cockpit is where the pilot sits to fly the plane.

5

Some planes have propellers and some planes have jet engines.

The propeller spins and changes the air pressure. This makes the plane lift and move forward.

This is a biplane. It has two long wings and one propeller.

This is a fixed wing propeller plane. It has one long wing. The wing is above the pilot.

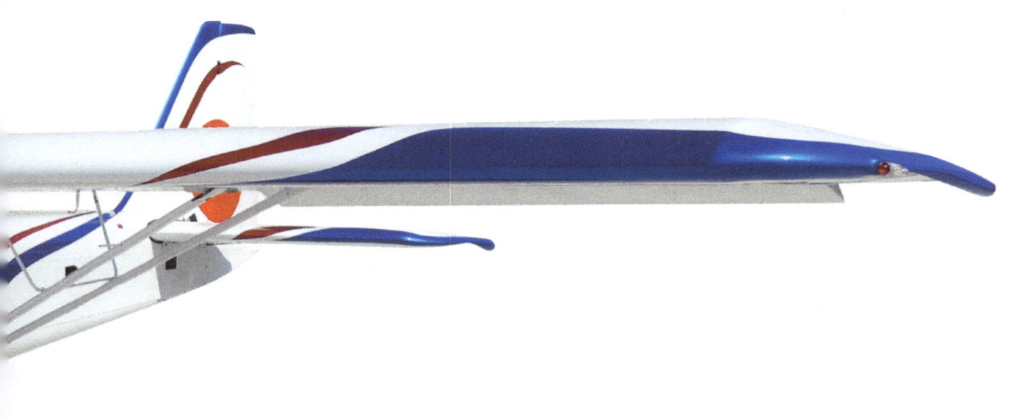

This is a low wing propeller plane. It has one long wing. The wing is below the pilot.

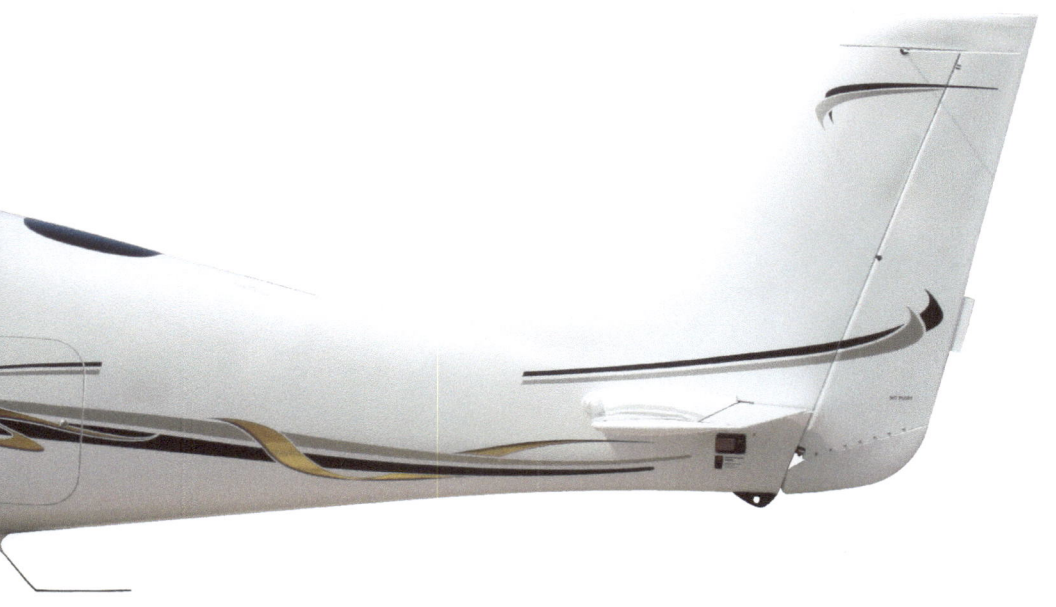

This is a twin engine plane.
It has two propellers.

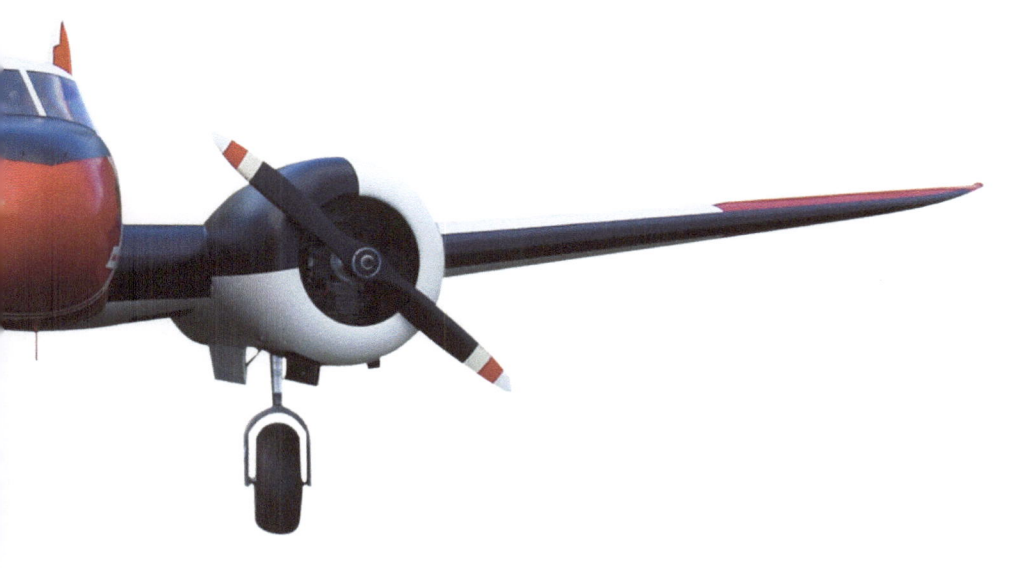

This is a Spitfire.
In World War II, pilots fought with this plane.

This is the nose of a jet.
It has no propellers.

22

This is a jumbo jet. Many people can ride on it. A jet like this can fly over oceans.

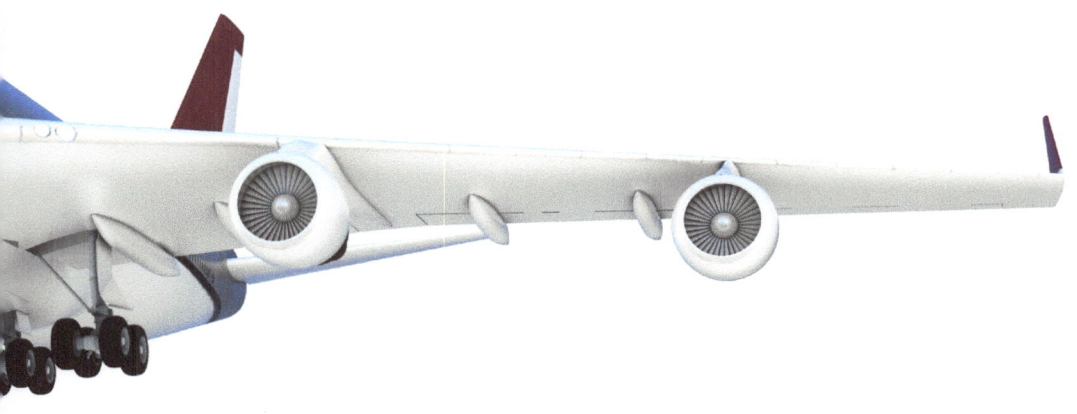

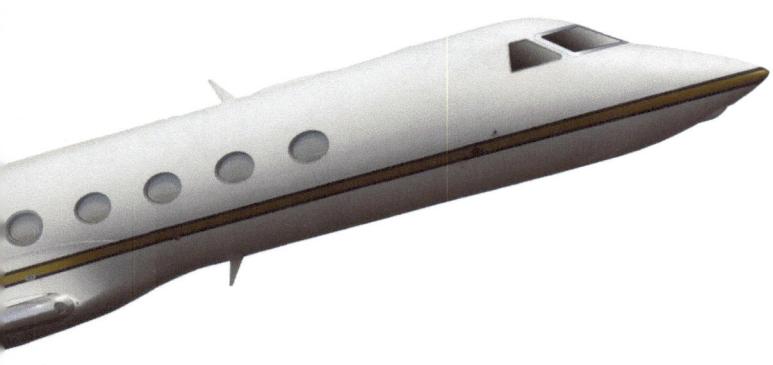

This is a private passenger jet. A small group of people can fly on a private jet.

This is a F-16 fighter jet. The pilot can see out of the cockpit because it is like a bubble.

This is an A-7 Corsair jet. Pilots thought it was slow and ugly, but it had better technology than faster planes.

This is a Yak-52. It has two seats. It was made in Russia to help pilots learn how to do tricks like loops and spins.

Airplanes help people, fight wars, travel and have fun. What kind of plane would you like to fly?

www.ingramcontent.com/pod-product-compliance
Lightning Source LLC
LaVergne TN
LVHW010020070426
835507LV00001B/14